SAHAJA YOGA

Shri Mataji Nirmala Devi

DIVINE COOL BREEZE BOOKS

SAHAJA YOGA
Shri Mataji Nirmala Devi

third edition 2018
© Nirmal Intellectual Property Corporation (NIPC)
All rights reserved

No part of this book may be used or reproduced
in any manner, printed or electronic,
without permission from the publisher.

front page photograph by Matthew Fogarty

ISBN 978-1-71696-004-8
Divine Cool Breeze book 20 (DCB020-SY)

Divine Cool Breeze Books
www.divinecoolbreeze.com

Innocence is an eternal quality
which can never be
lost or destroyed.

Contents

1. Sahaja Yoga 1

2. Vishwa Nirmala Dharma 29

3. Sahaja Culture 51

4. Sahaja Yogis 61

5. The Leader in Sahaja Yoga 73

6. Sahaja Yoga & Children 93

CHAPTER ONE

Sahaja Yoga

Saha means "with." *Ja* means "born." Yoga means union with the all-pervading power of divine love. This is a very subtle subject – absolutely valid and can be proved – of our ascent into higher awareness.

At the very outset, one has to be a seeker of truth and, with scientific attitude, one should approach the subject. It should be treated respectfully like a hypothesis and, if found by experiments as truth, should be accepted by honest people in the spirit of honesty because this is for one's total benevolence and for the benevolence of all the world.

This knowledge is of very ancient times and mostly comes from India. Of course, every religion has talked about our second birth and also about the tree of life. As the knowledge of science comes from the West, but is accepted by the East, why should such a knowledge of reality be denied? Why not at least heed to it seriously, when it is the knowledge of the roots of all our civilization and evolution? The nations have to think why the modern civilization is killing all human values. What we need is a careful introspection as to where we have gone wrong. Where did we miss out on our path of progress? How has this decadence crawled into our society? Why are some of us sick with frustration and insecurity? Why are some of the people of the progressive countries succumbing to physical and mental deterioration? Science has no answer. So let us take to spirituality. Why not ask a question? Is there any other power that controls the universe?

As described in the scriptures, there is an all-pervading power of God's love (*paramachaitanya*). It is a subtle power which does all living work and which cannot be felt at the level of human awareness. Sahaja Yoga means that a seeker of truth (*sadhaka*) has the birthright to get his Self-realization (*atma sakshat kar*) spontaneously. Self-realization or self-knowledge is the destination of human evolution and also of all the religions. This is the last breakthrough a human being has to achieve, for which there is a complete living machinery placed in the human spinal cord and in the brain. This machinery is being established step by step during our evolution. This living machinery works through its power, manifesting the parasympathetic and both sympathetic nervous systems. Whatever we achieve in evolution is expressed by our conscious mind through the central nervous system.

To connect us to this subtle energy, which permeates into every atom and molecule, there is a power of pure desire, which is placed in the sacrum bone of the human beings, which is called as *kundalini*. *Kundal* means "coils." It exists in three and a half coils. There is a divine mathematical coefficient about three and a half coils.

This triangular bone is called *sacrum*. That means that the people in Rome and Greece in the ancient times knew about this divine sacred power of kundalini. That is why they called this bone sacred. This sacrum bone is placed at the base of the spinal cord and is triangular in shape.

The kundalini is like a connecting cord, as is in every piece of electrical machinery, which connects the machinery to the main source of electricity. In the same way, when this energy of kundalini is awakened, threads (some of them) rise and ultimately connect the human being to the all-pervading power (*paramachaitanya*).

It is a spontaneous happening. It is a living process. The whole evolutionary process has been a living process and now a stage has come for human beings to have the last state of spiritual existence through Self-realization. A human being can be compared to a seed which is not active spiritually and has not started its living process of growth in spirituality, but, when it is embedded in the Mother Earth, Mother Earth has the power (with the help of water) to sprout the seed. In the same way, the kundalini can be awakened spontaneously by the power of Sahaja Yoga. When this kundalini rises, a new life process starts in the human awareness, resulting in the growth of spirituality. This spiritual life growth is a new state into which a human being starts growing in his innate divinity. This enlightens his physical, mental, emotional and spiritual being.

This living process is very clearly described in Indian scriptures since ancient times. There are 108 *Upanishadas* in the Sanskrit language which have exposed the knowledge about kundalini awakening and the spiritual ascent. It is also indicated in other scriptures of other countries. In the *Bible*, it is called the tree of life and it is quoted that "I will appear before you like tongues of flames." When the kundalini rises, she passes through various centres which look like tongues of flame when enlightened. The cool breeze of the Holy Ghost of Pentecost is this power that you can feel in Sahaja Yoga. The Gospel of St. Thomas very clearly describes the Sahaj experience as the ultimate of our religious life. Also it says we must look after our centres. This kundalini has to ascend and pierce through six solid centres, which are placed in the spinal cord and in the brain. The last breakthrough is the actualization of the "baptism," as one feels the cool breeze of the Holy Ghost emitting out of one's fontanelle bone area.

The first centre is called the *Mooladhara* centre. It has four petals (sub-plexuses), is placed below the triangular bone and is responsible on the physical level of the manifestation of the pelvic plexus, which looks after all our excretion, inclusive of sex activity. When the kundalini rises, then this centre becomes inactive in the excretion functions, but active in the support of the rising of the kundalini.

Though the kundalini has to rise through six centres, the first centre of Mooladhara protects the purity of chastity of the kundalini at the time of its awakening.

The Mooladhara centre is for our innocence and one should know that innocence can never be destroyed. It is indestructible, although it might be covered by lots of clouds due to perverted human sexual behaviour. Thinking or relating everything to sex, we become sex-oriented, reduced to sex points and our behaviour is no more humane, but becomes even worse than animals. Flirtation, housewives becoming prostitutes, homosexuals, lesbians, abuse of children by their parents, incestuous relations, etc., despite all arbitrary abandonment of natural laws, the innocence, the power of the Mooladhara remains, although in a sleeping or a sick state which can be cured and normalized through kundalini awakening. Innocence is the power that really supports the kundalini when it is rising and normalizing all the centres.

At the awakening of kundalini, this centre stops all other functions of the centre. Thus the physical functions, to cater to the pelvic plexus of excretion, are completely stopped. Thus, at that time, a seeker becomes innocent like a child.

In many people, one can see with the naked eye the rising of the kundalini, whenever there is obstruction in the higher centres. But if there is an obstruction in the second or third centre, one can see the triangular bone pulsating like a heart.

The second centre is the centre of *Swadisthana*. It has six petals and caters on the physical level to functions of the aortic plexus and is the one which supplies us with the energy of creativity, of thinking, of being futuristic. It supplies power to the brain cells by converting fat cells into brain cells.

The third centre is called as *Nabhi* centre and has ten petals. It is behind the navel, and this centre gives us the power to sustain something within ourselves.

On the physical level, it caters to the functions of the solar plexus.

The fourth centre is called as the *Anahat* chakra, meaning the heart centre. It has twelve petals and it is placed behind the sternum in the spinal cord. This centre produces the antibodies until the age of twelve years and then these antibodies are circulated into the whole body to be ready to fight any kind of attack on the body or on the mind. If there is any attack on the person, these antibodies are informed through the sternum, which has a remote control of information.

The fifth centre is called as the *Vishuddhi* chakra. This is placed in the neck of the human beings and it has sixteen petals, which look after the ears, nose, throat, neck, tongue, teeth, etc. This centre is responsible for communication with others because, through our eyes, through our nose, through our speech, through our hands, we communicate with others. On the physical level it caters to the cervical plexus.

The sixth centre is called the *Agnya* chakra and has only two petals. This is the centre placed where the two optic nerves cross each other in the brain (*optic chiasma*). This centre caters to the pituitary and pineal body, which manifest the two institutions of ego and superego within us.

Lastly, **the seventh centre**, the most important centre, is the Sahasrara, which has got, according to Sahaja Yoga, a thousand petals. Actually, there are a thousand nerves and, if you cut the transverse section of the brain, you can see that all these petal-like structures of the brain are forming a lotus of a thousand petals. This centre of a thousand petals covers the limbic area of the brain, before Realization, like a closed bud of a lotus. Above this are covering the balloon-like structures of the ego and superego. As the brain is covered completely when these two institutions join and calcification takes place on top of the head (*fontanelle bone* area), that is how we become a closed personality, like an egg. At the time of our awakening, of our second birth (resurrection), this egg-like personality breaks at the tip of the head. This is the reason, at the time of Easter, Christians offer eggs.

There is an "autonomous nervous system" working in our being. *Auto* means "self," so who is this auto who is running this autonomous nervous system? Doctors have called it a self-propelled system, but who is the Self?

The Self is the Spirit. This Spirit resides in the heart of every human being and is in a witness-like state. The spirit is the reflection of God Almighty, while the Kundalini is Primordial Mother or you can call it Adi Shakti, Holy Ghost or Athena. So the kundalini is the reflection of the Holy Ghost, while the Spirit is the reflection of God Almighty. The all-pervading power of love is the power of the Primordial Mother, which creates and evolves and does all the living work.

There are actually three channels in the system. The one in the centre is called *Sushumna*, which caters to the parasympathetic nervous system or the autonomous nervous system. The one on the left looks after the left sympathetic nervous system and on the right it looks after the right sympathetic nervous system. Now, it is not accepted yet or discovered yet in medical science that the left and right sympathetic nervous systems are two different juxtaposed systems. Their functions are absolutely opposite to each other.

The left side channel is called *Ida Nadi* and is connected to the right side and the back of the brain. The two left and right channels cross at the Agnya chakra level. This channel caters to the left sympathetic nervous system. This channel looks after our emotional life and our past. It is the channel which creates our past. Whatever is the present today becomes the past tomorrow. The subconscious mind receives information from this channel. The subconscious mind has an age-old collective subconscious mind beyond it. Everything that was in the past since Creation resides dormant in the collective subconscious. This collective subconscious has all that is dead in the evolutionary process collected and stored. Whatever is dead or gone out of the circulation of evolution and also whatever is spilling out of the subconscious mind goes out into the collective subconscious mind.

The right side channel is called as *Pingala Nadi*, which crosses Ida Nadi at the Agnya chakra level. It is connected with the left side and the front of the brain. This channel caters to the right sympathetic nervous system. On the right-hand side, there is the supraconscious mind, which creates our future. Whatever we think about our future is recorded on the right-hand side and it also has a collective supraconscious, which has got all that is dead, which happened due to over-ambitious, futuristic personalities, aggressive animals or plants.

The central path is called *Sushumna*, through which the kundalini passes to pierce through the fontanelle bone area (*brahmarandra*) to enter into the subtle energy of the all-pervading power. This is how the actualization of Self-realization (baptism) takes place. First, the hands feel, at the fontanelle bone area and on the fingertips, the cool breeze of the Holy Ghost. The hands are steady, they do not shake, they look normal, but the seeker feels the ripples of cool breeze. For the first time he feels the existence of the all-pervading power.

It is easy to deny, but no use for a real seeker of truth to deny that there is any such thing as an all-pervading power because one has not yet felt it. As already stated, one has to have a very open mind, like a scientist. Whatever may be the absolute truth for a saint, may not be for an ordinary human being. Still, one can keep one's mind open and see for one's self and, if it works out, then one would have an enlightened faith in Sahaja Yoga and not a blind faith.

As earnest, honest people, one must understand that this is for the transformation of all people who have been waiting for their ascent. All our problems come from human beings. If human beings are transformed into a new realm of reality, of collective consciousness, when they are aware of themselves (Self-knowledge) and also aware within themselves about others, as innate knowledge on their central nervous system, the entire problem of our personal, social, economic and political life will be solved. But for that, one has to become humble and should know that science cannot explain how the living process works. The principles of this power can only be understood when one feels this power after Self-realization.

Sahaja Yoga is not just a fashion, cult or alternative method. Thus, there is no organization, as such, in Sahaja Yoga. There is no membership in Sahaja Yoga, except that we had to have a nominal trust. By that trust, we have to operate for legal affairs, but Sahaja Yoga has no permanent list of names of people. There is no dead organization, but a living collective single organism. The body has the cells. After Self-realization, the spirits of the cells are enlightened by Sahaja

Yoga. The seeker's being has to actually be sprouted by kundalini awakening. Then becoming is important.

When the kundalini rises, one can feel easily the cool breeze coming out of one's fontanelle bone area on top of one's head. One can feel it on oneself and one has to certify oneself. One can also feel this cool breeze all around oneself. This cool breeze is the one that is manifested by the all-pervading power of divine love. For the first time in life, one actualizes the experience of feeling this subtle divine power. Even after feeling this power, one has to understand that this kundalini is not yet fully established. In ordinary mechanical language, we can say that the connection is not established. One has to work it out. Though sprouting in a seed is spontaneous, the gardener has to now look after the tender sapling. In the same way, a seeker has to look after his Self-realization in the beginning. Some people achieve heights easily, but some have to work for six or seven months and are still not all right. Under these circumstances, it is important that one must know and understand where the problem is by understanding the proper decoding system and its practices in Sahaja Yoga.

Thus, the human being rises above all the shackles of slavery. One does not need any more guidance from any guru. One becomes one's own master, no longer groping in the dark for support. One becomes an absolutely free person. No one can intimidate or manipulate a Sahaja Yogi. People come to Sahaja Yoga from many sects, religious organizations and schools of thought, but their conditionings drop off. No one can condition a realized soul after Sahaja Yoga.

This freedom is very beautiful and then slowly one learns to fly like a bird on one's own until one masters it and knows all about divinity.

After Sahaja Yoga, the personality rises so much above others and the sense of discretion becomes so sharp and perfect that the media, television, entrepreneurs, fake masters, misguiding or modern methods, nothing can deviate the mind from the righteous path.

No one can lead a Sahaja Yogi astray, unless and until a Sahaja Yogi himself falls into some temptation, fear or manipulation.

The Sahaja Yogi enjoys his freedom and that of other Sahaja Yogis. He knows his powers and has knowledge about himself. He becomes a powerful, free saint leading an angelic life.

At the very beginning of this happening, one starts feeling on one's fingertips the problems on the centres. One has to just decode the feelings that one gets on one's own fingertips and has to also know the practice that would solve these problems. The fingertips are the ending of the left and right sympathetic nervous systems. They become enlightened as they reflect the subtle centres.

By using this method, there have been so many people who have been cured completely of very serious, incurable ailments like blood cancer, etc. There are two doctors in Delhi University who have already got M.D. degrees for curing incurable diseases and there is one more who is also completing her thesis about Sahaja Yoga. There are seven doctors in London, three in Australia and one in Taiwan who are trying to record all those who have been cured through Sahaja Yoga practices. It does not only solve physical problems, but mental and spiritual problems. There are many mental cases who have been cured with Sahaja Yoga. There are some doctors who are now in charge of mental hospitals because of their expertise in Sahaja Yoga. We have two psychiatrists very highly placed. One is in charge of seven hospitals in London and one is the dean of a faculty of psychology in Riyadh. There are many other doctors and Sahaja Yogis who are curing through Sahaja Yoga all over the world. It must be mentioned that Sahaja Yoga is not for curing people, but for achieving Self-realization. Thus, as a by-product, one gets physical, mental and spiritual well-being in totality.

There are also many people who have given up their bad habits of smoking, drinking and drugs, sometimes overnight. So many people who were drug addicts have given up drugs because they have found that power of the Spirit within themselves that helps them to enjoy their own being and also gives them power to stop them running after these enjoyments which are very transitory, have had reactions and are destructive in the long run. It is not a rational or mental understanding, but the light of the Self which gives power and expels the darkness spontaneously. Many people who are being harmed by false gurus, cults and anti-cults are absolutely cured and have become very great people in their own fields. So many have achieved great heights in their accomplishments. The ex-president of the Hague High Court, the late Dr. Najendra Singh, was a Sahaja Yogi.

Apart from physical, mental and emotional problems, we have much wider problems in our society. It is caused by a lack of balance and wisdom and no sense of collectivity.

The first problem is of children and the family. We have many marriages in Sahaja Yoga and it is quite surprisingly noteworthy that, in all these years, there are very few divorces among those people who got married in Sahaja Yoga. Moreover, the children of these people are mostly born-realized souls. They are the ones who are special people who have come on this Earth at this time and having selected their parents as Sahaja Yogis. One can feel the cool breeze coming out of their fontanelle bone area or from their body just after their birth. They have a very joyous, serene expression and their eyes are sparkling at the time of birth.

The effects of Sahaja Yoga act on agriculture through the divine cool breeze (vibrations). Many farmers and specialists of agriculture have experimented and found that the crop that grows out of non-hybrid seeds, which are being vibrated with the divine power of the cool breeze, sometimes grows eight or ten times more than the hybrid seeds, for which one has to pay so much to some organization all the time, because hybrid seeds have no power to regenerate. The experiments were carried out very extensively by Dr. Hamid of Austria and by Dr. Sangwe of Nasik.

It also helps ecological problems in a big way because man becomes extremely balanced and doesn't use things which are not required for him, nor does he make machinery work in such a way that it creates an imbalance and dominates him. Sahaja Yoga has also been successful in combating acid rain in some forests of Austria.

Ordinary Sahaja Yogis can become personalities who are Sahaj doctors and Sahaj scientists and can create them out of other human beings because they have powers to give Realization to others and also to cure others. As one light enlightens another light, Sahaja Yoga goes on spreading in all kinds of areas. As this is a living, invaluable process, you cannot pay for it. Also the knowledge (*gyana*) which makes you a Sahaja Yogi (*gnostic*) is given absolutely free of charge.

Now Sahaja Yoga is followed in more than one hundred nations. There is no money that can be paid for this living process. That is why so many false gurus, who are making money, and cults and anti-cults, who are trying to project some sort of false image just to make money, are all very much against Sahaja Yoga. They are not against each other. But they should also understand that this is the golden age of emancipation, resurrection and last judgement. If we can achieve, all of us, including them also, it will have the blessing of the divine love, which has been promised a long time back.

There are some new mushroom organizations called anti-cults, which have no knowledge, no legal authority or legal right, who have come up and are just making money. They are another type of cult. The people who have suffered in those cults and anti-cults have all been helped in the thousands by Sahaja Yoga.

A human being has got ten valences of humanity built within, which, when enlightened through kundalini awakening, make him a very balanced, righteous and a really, innately, religious person. One may follow any religion outwardly, but one is still quite capable of committing any sin or murdering someone or doing something which is very hurtful or dangerous for society. Some may be righteous out of fear or from family conditionings. Of course, there are many who are honestly devoted or very innocent, who follow these religions, but they do not know that these religions were created for one to ascend into higher realms of spirituality. But a Sahaja Yogi, once his innate religion is awakened, becomes a person who has such a balance and wisdom as part and parcel of his being that he can never think of committing any sin or doing something which is arbitrary or making somebody miserable or killing someone.

Such a person can only be a yogi who is united with the all-pervading divine power. He is called as a Sahaja Yogi because he has all the knowledge of sahaj (spontaneous) kundalini awakening. He knows spontaneously how to awaken the kundalini. He knows all about his inner machinery, his own Spirit and of the kundalini state of all others who are not yogis. He also knows, as the truth which is proven, about the power of love of the Primordial Mother, the Holy Ghost.

Because of this, he is innately a very compassionate, dynamic, contented, confident person.

Sahaja Yogis are now expressing the dynamism of their values and life in different areas all over the world. There is also a very beautiful, compassionate, loving relationship working together in all the Sahaja Yogis of all the nations. There are some business people who were completely stunned by the opposition of the labour in their businesses. With Sahaja Yoga, the labour and the master relationship has improved so much that they are regarded as the most successful businessmen. Business has improved and people are working like one family and really enjoying working with such Sahaja Yogi business people.

Creativity in literature, like poetry, drama, novels and writings, is absolutely miraculously working in some people, so that people who never knew a word of the Urdu language have started composing beautiful lyrics in that language. The same with music. There are some very great artists who have become very big names because they were blessed by the Adi Shakti. They say that, with the blessings of Sahaja Yoga, they have risen so much higher in the realm of music. In the field of art, there are some Sahaja Yogis who, after coming to Sahaja Yoga, have become renowned in art. Also surprisingly, people have improved economically. In England, where unemployment is formidable, you cannot find a single unemployed Sahaja Yogi.

All these things are worldly achievements. By the blessing of the divine power, Sahaja Yogis are blessed with the wisdom and the balance that are within them. But above all, what Sahaja Yogis get is the powerful attention that penetrates into any areas and acts. This means that if a Sahaja Yogi puts his attention onto somebody, it acts and tries to help that person to get over his problems without doing anything outwardly. This attention is so beautiful that, from the beginning, it indicates clearly on one's central nervous system, on one's fingertips, the different centres of other people and also one's own. These signals are decoded already and one can verify the decoding. If one knows how to cure or correct those centres, one can help other people very well. Moreover, as a Sahaja Yogi becomes an egoless personality, he does not feel that he has done something to oblige someone. Sahaja Yoga is the pure love of God which is living and invaluable. No money can be charged for this cure or for kundalini awakening.

It makes one very dynamic and one is not afraid of standing for the truth and no one can manipulate them. Sahaja Yogis have met even some honest, intelligent journalists who came to Sahaja Yoga. They have been extremely positive and are standing only for real truth and not just for sensational falsehood. These are modern days of corruption and delusion (*Kali Yuga*). When falsehood becomes the nature of human beings, they destroy all higher values in the mud of money and assumed powers. These money-blinded people believe in satanic methods of harming good people with lies, false scandals and vulgarity.

There are Sahaja Yogis who are in the areas of teaching or running schools. These people are doing marvellous work. They have handled some very difficult children and moulded them into such beautiful personalities. It is amazing how their divine love has brought forth such an advancement in these children who were supposed to be very dangerously violent. Of course, some hard nuts could not be tackled. With Sahaja Yoga, many children who were very dull in class have become alert and intelligent and showing great results in their studies. Even difficult exams like chartered accountancy, architecture, engineering and medicine are passed in record time, with flying colours, by Sahaja Yogis.

Sahaja Yoga is for the emancipation of the whole world at every level. Once we have people of a certain number in Sahaja Yoga, it will start triggering understanding of real righteousness, religiousness and our love for God and enlightened faith in God. This is how the resurrection time is going to be worked out. This is the last judgement time and everyone can judge himself or herself through the light of the Spirit. The knowledge of Sahaja Yoga cannot be described in a few sentences or one small book, but one should understand that all this great work of creation and evolution is done by some great subtle organization, which is in the great divine form.

The human being which is like a divine computer, only has to be plugged into the mains. Modern Sahaja Yoga has achieved a new method by which en masse Realization can be given. In Russia, we used to get fourteen thousand people in a stadium for a program, and ninety percent of them got Realization at every meeting. So this is a great achievement in these days of chaos. Educated Russians are very introspective and very open-minded, very scientific by temperament and they just want to know something that is beyond human comprehension.

Despite the chaotic conditions of the world, these are special times. Sahaja Yoga can be called as Maha Yoga because it is working on such a mass scale. At the time of Shri Rama only one, Nachiketa, got his Realization, but today there are thousands and thousands who have mastered Sahaja Yoga.

Definitely our creator, God Almighty, is anxious to save the world from its destruction. Thus, he is working through the power of his desire, which is the Primordial Mother, (Adi Shakti, Holy Ghost, Athena).

The *brahmachaitanya* (all-pervading power) has itself become very active as a new type of age called *Krita Yuga* has started. It is achieving results and producing miracles. It is not only talk or reading scriptures, but it is actualization and the proof. Of course, all false people are afraid of facing the truth because Sahaja Yoga goes against their interests. They are challenging and opposing violently the spread of Sahaja Yoga. The *Satya Yuga* has to be established by the Sahaja Yogis. Now they are not alone like Christ, our Lord, Mohammed, the Prophet, Socrates, the philosopher, or other incarnations, seers and realized souls.

They are in thousands. They are not in any way hampered by a few people who are trying to harm their collective process. The truth will be established and thus the dawn of *Satya Yuga* (the kingdom of God) can be seen on the horizon. The message of Sahaja Yoga is that even these negative people have to accept the truth and enjoy the blessings of divine love.

CHAPTER TWO

Vishwa Nirmala Dharma

Vishwa means "universe," *Nirmala* means "pure, immaculate" and *Dharma* means "religion."

Within human beings lies the dormant power of pure desire (*kundalini*) which is the reflection of the Primordial Mother or Holy Ghost. All other desires are not pure because they do not give satisfaction. One of the principles of economics is that in general wants are not satiable, that human beings run from one desire to another desire. Whether one is aware or not, one is seeking satisfaction or joy. One may seek joy in money, in possessions, in power or in human love, but is lost in the wilderness of the duality of happiness and unhappiness.

In every human heart resides the Spirit (*Atma*) which is the reflection of God Almighty (*parameshwara*).

The nature of the kundalini is that it is the power of pure desire. She is an individual mother of every individual and she is the one who is dormant and waiting for a proper time to give every individual his or her second birth. She is like a tape which has a record of all the good deeds (*punyas*), all the wrong doings, all the desires and aspirations of the individual. She is like a primula in a dormant seed. Once she is awakened and is connected to the all-pervading power, the spiritual growth of the fourth dimension (*turiya*) starts.

The nature of the Spirit is that it is a universal being within every individual. As there is one God Almighty, His reflection on every human heart is the same, but the reflection of the Spirit varies because of the different types of reflectors. When this Spirit, which is the source of joy and truth, is connected through the kundalini, the human attention becomes enlightened. Thus, one knows the absolute truth on one's central nervous system and becomes a joyous collective being. The Spirit is reflected in the heart, but the seat of God Almighty is above the fontanelle bone area, above the apex of the head.

After this living force of kundalini is connected to the all-pervading divine power within a human being, it starts developing the spirituality of a person. One touches the spirituality within oneself and grows into another dimension, the fourth one. Thus a saintly and wise personality develops. This personality is the one which is unfolding itself naturally, spontaneously (*sahaja*), but also, by knowing how to handle this all-pervading power through the knowledge of purity (*shuddha vidya*), one can evolve in a much faster way into that new dimension.

Once the Spirit starts shining fully in one's attention one actually becomes enlightened in the sense that you can see for yourself that you become your own guide. One becomes one's own master. Then you don't need any guide, but you are the master of yourself. In the past, this process was limited to one or to very few persons, but now a phenomenon to allow en masse Realization has been discovered.

All such enlightened people follow a religion which is called as *Vishwa Nirmala Dharma*, meaning the innate pure religion within us. These people have actualized the enlightenment. They have actualized the baptism because they feel the cool breeze as the kundalini pierces through the fontanelle and, thus, have become religious saints, yogis, yoginis and seers. They are not like ordinary people who have not entered into the new fourth dimension of awareness and established themselves. These are the people who know themselves within and know others in collective consciousness. They are the people who have achieved a state in which they know on their central nervous system that they are part and parcel of the whole. It is not a blind faith or lip service building a net of empty words (*shabda jalam*).

This is the subtle knowledge of the roots. All the trees of modern civilization have grown outside. If we do not go to our roots and find out the fundamentals of our existence, these unbalanced, crazily expanded civilizations are going to be destroyed. It is very important and imminent that the world should try to take its attention towards finding its roots. It is described in every Indian scripture. India is a very ancient country and it has been blessed by many seers and saints who wrote treatises about reality and guidelines on how to achieve it. Like all other real saints of the world they also suffered at the hands of people of outward religions (*dharma martandas*).

The writings of these enlightened souls are mostly in Sanskrit and were not available to the general public. Whenever translated, they were not even mentioning kundalini awakening as the only way to achieve Self-realization. It was completely deleted when translated. It was in the twelfth century that a great incarnation of a saint, Sri Gyaneshwara (god of knowledge) was born. He lived for only twenty three years. There were three brothers and one sister. All of them were tortured by the people in charge of religion (*dharma-martandas*). Gyaneshwara took the permission of his *guru* (master), who was his eldest brother, and wrote in the regional language a book called *Gyaneshwari*. In the sixth chapter, he clearly wrote about kundalini, but again the dharma-martandas said that this chapter was not allowed to be read (*nishiddha*).

Then came the *tantrikas* who did not know anything about the kundalini, the instrument (*yantra*), also they did not know anything about how it works (*tantra*). They practised all black arts and indulged into immoral practices of violence and sex.

When the kundalini is awakened the ten valences (the ten commandments) are awakened within. The religion becomes innate and our whole priorities change because religion in Sahaja Yoga is the ultimate of every religion of any form. It is not limited to one religion, but it has the best of all religions. All real religions are leading to one aim, to one goal. That goal is to achieve Self-knowledge through our second birth. In the Sanskrit language, a bird is called as a *dwija*, twice born, because first it is an egg, then it has its second birth. In the same way, a person who is enlightened and has known the *brahma* (all-pervading power) is also known as dwija.

This dharma, which is innate within us, is awakened, by which they know that all the religions have come out of one source of spirituality. Anybody might come from any religion to Sahaja Yoga. They all know that we belong to one religion and that is the principle of all the religions. So there is no possibility of fundamentalism amongst Sahaja Yogis. There is no fighting or quarrelling. Everybody can see very clearly whatever religions they have followed so far, where they have deviated and what wrong they have been doing. Also, they are capable of correcting these things very easily. In India, there are Sahaja Yogis who are trying to work out the superstitions and caste systems. In the same way, in so many countries, people are trying to work out and eradicate wrong types of religious practices.

There are certain practices of this divine religion which keep the religion alive and active within. These are to be understood. The modus operandi, also how the kundalini is kept properly connected to the all-pervading power, and why these practices are important is explained. There are also proper methods of meditation for nourishment of the personality and how one could be in meditation all the time. Finally, you do not have to do the meditation, but you have to be in meditation the whole time. Now, all the knowledge comes to you from the Divinity and this knowledge is absolutely pure knowledge. It cannot be challenged. It cannot be changed. It is a permanent, eternal flow of knowledge. All this can be proved and verified.

There is a state of thoughtless awareness which you achieve, in which you are in contact with the present. All your thoughts are coming from your past or from your future, but you are not in the present. When you are in the present, you are silent and in the present only, spiritual growth takes place. Then inspiration comes to you as thought. Many people have been blessed by this inspiration and have created great works of art, music, dance and drama. Apart from that, these inspirations have helped many people in business, in politics and in economics. The same inspiration has created pure religion.

So one has to realize how this ascent into that peaceful area of complete security works and to enjoy your own values, your own status as a yogi. But a yogi is never an egoist. He never boasts about his state. On the contrary, he is extremely humble and helps everyone to come up to that state. Such a person is always concerned about the well-being of the whole world. This concern comes as his dharma, his religion, which is not forced upon him, but is innate within him, so that he works in that way. He cannot commit sin because he has a personality now which is sinless, which abhors sin. In this evolutionary process, now he has developed a sense of repulsion from something that is sinful or wrong. This sort of personality will change the whole world. We have had many such great people before, but most of them were alone with nobody to support them, so they were crucified, they were given poison, they were ill-treated by the general people who were blind. But nowadays, we have so many Sahaja Yogis. They may be attacked, but the day will come when they will be able to show to the world what they have achieved and what the whole world has to achieve.

Sahaja Yoga gives one the sensitivity of spirituality to innately know who is really a spiritual personality and who is a fake. It also gives one the sensitivity to know what is the suffering of another person and what is lacking in oneself. One becomes one's own judge. This is the last judgement, where one is going to judge oneself. The kundalini is going to be the judge. After this judgement only, human beings will be selected as the people who have achieved the state of Self-realization and those who have not.

The enlightened people were called as *gnostics*. This comes from the Sanskrit word *gna*, which means knowledge. But knowledge does not mean what one knows through the brain because the brain or intelligence takes one to rationality, which has no wisdom behind it. Rationality can take one anywhere, can justify anything, as it is not absolute. So one has to go beyond rationality, develop a higher sense of divinity by which one can understand the real problems and the actual solution of all these problems.

One has to understand that this religion is the essence of all the religions. It is the only religion that gives the real experience within oneself, which puts into a person that sensitivity for spirituality which cannot be got out of any number of lectures, sermons or books. Thus, a Sahaja Yogi knows and respects all the incarnations and saints.

If we have to change this world and if we have to save our people from complete destruction, we have to take to wisdom and that is only possible when the brain is enlightened by the kundalini. This is what is very important today, when we see that this world is on the verge of destruction. Of course, the Creator Himself is very anxious to save us and that is why He has, in these modern times, which are called *Kali Yuga*, made the all-pervading power activated.

So, now a new age has started which is called the Age of Aquarius (*kumbha*), meaning the pitcher, carrier of spiritual holy water, that is the work of the kundalini. The activity of the kundalini is like the sap of the tree and does not get stuck at one flower (centre). Moreover, these are special times. This is the resurrection time. The last judgement is done by the kundalini. On the fingertips, one can feel oneself and can judge oneself. Moreover, the all-pervading power has become very activated, so the Kali Yuga (modern times) is passing into *Krita Yuga of Brahmachaitanya* (activated all-pervading power). This is helping the en-masse enlightenment and Self-realization. After this will be *Satya Yuga* (the age of truth). We have to take advantage of this activity of the brahmachaitanya by all the time being connected with the all-pervading power and achieving Realization and establishing it. After such a state, a person becomes very dynamic and compassionate. His race, sex, nationality and age do not hamper his dynamic life.

There are so many blessings in Sahaja Yoga that it is impossible to compile them into a book as it would require volumes and volumes to assemble the experiences of the Sahaja Yogis.

Whatever one is doing now is relative in this modern world. In relative terms, everything is working itself out. This relative working is not going to give any absolute results. Absolute knowledge only comes from the Spirit and so, unless we know the Self, the Spirit, we cannot know what is absolute and what is absolute truth. Otherwise, when we live in the relative world, we will be always quarrelling, fighting and having wars. But if one is in the absolute, then one knows that there is only one truth for everything and there will be no more arguments or discussions. Everybody will enjoy that truth, as it is absolute.

All theories, like communism and capitalism, will fail because they are not in the centre. When one is in the centre, one becomes the greatest capitalist because one has all the powers and one becomes the greatest communist because one has to share them with others. One has to give it to others and that is the only way one can enjoy one's own powers. If one does not share them with others, one will never enjoy whatever one has achieved. One of the biggest problems of the intellectuals is that they never want to accept anything as absolute, but they always want to find alternatives for everything. Now there is no alternative for one's ascent. As a seed has to grow its primule, so the kundalini has to be awakened. But some of those who have come to Sahaja Yoga have also gone away, saying that there must be some other methods and powers that should work it out. This is just an escapist reaction. Supposing you are digging a well and you find water in one place, what is the use of digging in other places? Whatever you have found, it is the water, so why not make the well there? But this is how many people are escaping reality. One should face it and get it. There is no other way human transformation can take place, as has been said in so many ancient books. Still, if people want to escape it, then you cannot help them and force them. You cannot in any way condemn them.

So the problem remains: how to make these people know that this is a living process, which has already started, is working in so many people when they have no other alternative. They should become Sahaja Yogis. Actually, one requires tremendous patience with these people because they can be saved if they understand that it is for their benevolence, it is for their good. After coming to Sahaja Yoga, very few people have suffered from any serious diseases and there are so many who have never been to a doctor or to a dentist. It is also for one's mental peace. So many of them have written to me that they have found their mental peace at long last. There are so many who write how they have achieved proficiency and balance in their work.

But all this does not convince certain people because they always want to escape. This character of escaping is keeping out many people who are quite deserving. They are very good people, very nice people, but, because of this escapist nature, they cannot get to Sahaja Yoga. Sahaja Yogis are extremely kind and extremely wise. I am sure one day that all such people who are trying to escape will also understand that it is not only for their personal benevolence, but for the benevolence of the whole world. Somehow, when it comes to religion, they will only follow Christ or only follow Mohammed Sahib or only follow Buddha. In Sahaja Yoga, we have all of them, absolutely activating your kundalini. Everybody in Sahaja Yoga knows so much about them and the most important thing is that they are all with us, they are part and parcel of us and they are not separated by anything. They were working the same process in history and now we are working it out in the present with all of them.

Some of the seekers have another problem. It has become like a momentum of seeking in their life that they are seekers. They do not know how to stop and they want to go on seeking eternally. This is another problem for people to understand, that the time has come for you to stop and introspect yourself. Even if God comes and stands before them, they will say, "Oh, we are seeking God, do you know anything about God or not?"

It has been found that those who have a superior type of intelligence take to Sahaja Yoga very fast. Most of the people we have now in Sahaja Yoga are extremely intelligent. Some of them are professors in universities. But intelligence can cheat itself. What is needed is the intelligence of wisdom. It is a kind of special intelligence which just makes them understand that this is the truth. It has been found in many countries, like Columbia, Russia or Bulgaria, that people just saw the photograph and they felt that this is the truth. It amazed us how they could see truth in a photograph. Thousands and thousands of them were there at the meetings. They had a kind of spiritual sensitivity to appearances. I am not like any cinema actress and in no way am I any pompous guru. I am a normal housewife, but, despite that, how could they find out that there is something spiritual about me? It is remarkable that some people have this gift that they can just feel the spirituality. I am sure that the new generation that is coming up will have that sensitivity much more developed.

Despite all these problems, Sahaja Yoga is spreading slowly and working out with great success so many miraculous things.

Also there are people in charge of religions (*dharma martandas*) who are only money-oriented, like mafias in the name of God, who spread and say false things about Sahaja Yoga. One should not get disappointed or upset if some people create trouble or try to disturb us. One should also not worry too much about the media. For example, some of the media in countries like Italy, Russia, Bulgaria, Colombia, India, Taiwan and Nepal are extremely sensitive and helpful.

There are countries where the media is seeking sensationalism. Sahaja Yoga is the greatest sensation. It is such a unique discovery, but to them it is more important to show some sort of vulgar thing because they have to make money and they think people will read more about things that are sensational. It is all right if they want to give this kind of news, but I still do not understand why they should criticize us and try to use us for their sensational trips. This could land them into great difficulties for telling lies if we take to the law and they will have to be careful before they make all such remarks, which have no foundation in reality. Still, a Sahaja Yogi should take a very, very mild approach to all such criticism and should know that they are all like blind men, trying to talk about an elephant and leading everyone into darkness.

Our work is of tremendous value. It is higher than any other work so far done in any other field in the world.

We have to stick to truth, to virtues, to our ideals. I always give the example of a sari, that if one end of the sari is stuck to a nail, whatever gale there may be, and whatever speed of the gale, still we can save the sari. In the same way, as long as we people keep to our purest values of spiritual life and try to discover the beauty of our own being, gradually people will see your extraordinary eminence. Your special qualities as Sahaja Yogis will show. They will definitely turn around, compare their lives with yours and will join in Sahaja Yoga to enjoy the divine vibrations. Sahaja Yoga is the only way the world can be saved and we have to understand our identity. This is a spiritual revolution, but you do not have to sacrifice anything. You have to just enjoy.

We are all concerned about sharing this great joy and helping people to ascend, but there is a snag in Sahaja Yoga, that you cannot just be a member of Sahaja Yoga. You have to face yourself and become a Sahaja Yogi, which I think people do not want to do. But there are lots of people who are of the right calibre. They have seen your courage and the innate power that you have to stand for those great values. I am sure that once they see how this power can empower them to change themselves and that this power can also empower them to give Realization to others and challenge others, they will understand that the meaning of their lives, the purpose of their lives is to be the instruments of God Almighty.

The collective content and feelings are very important in Vishwa Nirmala Dharma, which is working and is expressed mostly in a collective way. Formerly, in ancient times, there were only one or two enlightened people. They used to achieve their enlightenment individually. In these modern times, a method of en masse Realization has been found so in these modern times of resurrection a person cannot grow spiritually if he is not in the collective. It is not a mental understanding, but one develops collective consciousness as a new dimension of awareness in Sahaja Yoga, which is to be practised and verified in the collective. The collective must be respected and protected.

The collective is not to be used for any business.

The collective should not allow any one member to borrow or lend money to another member or to exploit another member in any way.

The collective should not allow any one member to go against any other member or against the leader, but the world leader can be informed directly.

The collective should not collect any money or spend it without the sanction of the world leader. All accounts must be kept and be made known to the collective. It should be in legal money and should be audited.

Anyone who is still having smoking, drinking, sex or mental problems should be kept out of the collective. They can attend only the public meetings.

Everyone should be open and clear-cut about Sahaja Yoga in the collective. Nothing should be secret or hidden.

No one should judge another member of the collective, but should judge himself.

Elders must be respected and looked after.

Children are the members of the international Sahaja Yoga family. They are the trust of all the Sahaja Yogis of the world. Their problems must be solved on a global basis.

In the collective, all must transcend the false barriers of race, colour, creed, nationality and fundamentalism. The foundation of the collective is divine love and respect.

The collective should be responsible for the books, video and audio tapes, which can be distributed to the deserving members.

Newsletters, containing globally important Sahaja Yoga news, can be sent to the collective centre, which can distribute them as they like.

Money can be charged for books, tapes, magazines, audio and videotapes, rings, pendants, medals, badges and seminars and tours.

Money cannot be charged for divine cures and Self-realization. The leaders could be paid for their travels if they are not working. The teachers and the managers of the schools must be paid the authorized salary.

Everyone should work in the collective efforts of arranging public meetings.

The collective should not allow dirty books and movies. It should not allow anyone to shout or to use dirty language.

Hugging and kissing between anyone should not be allowed. Between husband and wife there should be no romantic behaviour in public.

In the meetings, men should sit on one side and women on the other.

The collective should not allow anyone to form a group on any basis whatsoever.

The collective must physically support each other in discussions and not the negative or non-Sahaja Yogis.

The collective should be very gentle, kind and respectful to other seekers who are not yet in Sahaja Yoga.

The door of the Vishwa Nirmala Dharma is open to all. There is no conversion or initiation for Sahaja Yoga.

If Vishwa Nirmala Dharma is attacked, all the Sahaja Yogis from all over the world must fight.

The collective should research the scriptures and books written by enlightened souls and should produce books supporting Vishwa Nirmala Dharma.

The collective should have full knowledge and alertness about the forces acting against the ascent through Vishwa Nirmala Dharma.

CHAPTER THREE

Sahaja Culture

A simple thing like personal cleanliness: a Sahaja Yogi will always wash his face with running water and never from stagnating water or from a washbasin. Also, even if he takes a tub bath, he will use a shower afterwards. It is very important to cleanse the body very well.

Secondly, the other parts of the body, like the teeth, nose, the eyes, the hands, have to be kept very clean.

It is not necessary for every Sahaja Yogi to have a thin, bony structure. Some are thin, some are fat, some are medium-sized. It is all depending on the requirement of a personality and whatever is required, whatever is missing, all these things can be established properly in proper balance through Sahaja Yoga.

The foods that Sahaja Yogis eat must be vibrated and should be according to the needs of the body. For example, a person who is right-sided, who is very futuristic, who thinks too much, such a person will eat more carbohydrates, while a person who is not active, who is not so futuristic, will take more to proteins. There is no binding force that a particular type of food is suitable to all of them. It depends on everybody's nature (*prakriti*).

This culture makes a person automatically very soft natured. The culture where "to see and be seen" is the fundamental attitude just vanishes and a person who follows this culture is not bothered as to what others have to say about such a yogi. The only thing is that he does not go in some sort of funny, lousy dress or into some sort of unusual tantrums. He is the most normal person, leads a very dignified and serene life.

A Sahaja Yogi is not at all a lazy person. He doesn't go to the Himalayas, he doesn't give up his work, but he stays wherever he belongs. He tries to improve the conditions around him and he tries with his willpower of divine love to bring blessings on the people who are dependant on him and also he works for his country and for the world. He becomes a personality that is now ready to give to others and not to take from others.

So a person who is a mean person or who is miserly cannot fit into Sahaj culture. A person who is generous with others, kind to others, who is not money-oriented is a Sahaja Yogi. We have described already what a Sahaja Yogi should be, but the Sahaja culture is such that argumentation, unnecessary commentaries are not part of Sahaj culture.

Sahaj culture is to enjoy everything in its pure form. For example, in Sahaja culture, nobody is to flirt with anybody's wife or husband. You have to be a dedicated husband and wife. If you do not want to carry on with your spouse with some good reason, then, of course, Sahaja Yoga permits divorce, but it takes place very rarely.

We have to respect our elders, our parents, even if they don't understand Sahaja Yoga. We must forgive them because they are blind.

The Sahaja Yogis must respect their children. The teachers must also respect the children. If the children are extremely difficult, then the parents can sometimes slap them, but not the teachers. No teacher is allowed to, in any way, punish the child in such a way that the child gets hurt.

The house of a Sahaja Yogi should be like a lotus where even a beetle, which has got lots of thorns on its body, is welcome and is allowed to sleep for the whole night. A Sahaja Yogi's heart should be like a lotus which is pink, showing a very hospitable, sweet joyous temperament. He should always give to the people who are in need if he has much more and he should always protect people who are dependant on him.

He should not try to show off with his wealth. If he has a very big car or if he has some convenience of mobility, then he should ask other Sahaja Yogis to share it. If he has a very big house, he should ask other Sahaja Yogis to share it with him. But, he should not share with people who are not Sahaja Yogis because all such people might only try to exploit the person. But a Sahaja Yogi does not believe in exploitation. He is extremely kind to others and, if somebody is kind to a Sahaja Yogi, he tries to repay it by some way or the other. There is no question of obliging anyone or putting obligations on anyone.

The language of a Sahaja Yogi is very beautiful and one has to talk in such a manner that another person feels the joy of oneness.

These days of horrible ideas about sex are to be abhorred in Sahaj culture. Children are to be forgiven much more than anybody else and have to be taken into the fold. They may be illegitimate, they may be the ones who are being abused, they may be the ones who are being rejected by society. If there are some children who are extremely violent and pernicious, such children can be kept outside Sahaja Yoga with their parents.

In Sahaja Yoga we have no hierarchy. There are no priests. Everyone is equally the same. But only for contact's sake, we have leaders and these leaders have to be the best among the people they lead, the best Sahaja Yogis of the highest level. This method of appointing leaders is in a way absolutely mythical. Some leaders became greedy or carried on with bad habits. They had to leave, even if they try to do false propaganda. This is the only way one can keep in contact with the large groups, so it has to be accepted and be worked out, but not according to money, position or education, but according to Sahaj life.

Sahaja Yogis do not waste their energies or money on nonsensical things. They do not drink. They do not smoke. They do not take drugs.

The ladies do not waste their money in beauty parlours. This happens to them. Nobody tells them not to do it, but they just don't do it. They do not see vulgar films. They do not read vulgar things. They are noble, dignified, a special type of very purified people.

As far as the law is concerned, there are certain absurd laws with loopholes which give permission to people to do wrong things, but Sahaja Yogis do not accept those laws and never use the loopholes for their own purposes.

A materialistic society is never the ideal for Sahaja Yogis. It is the spiritual society which has the Spirit enlightening them and which is giving them all these joyous experiences of the miraculous powers of all-pervading Divine love. The ideals of Sahaja Yoga are very different.

The Spirit is the one which is the collective being within us. We do not have to start an organization to call it something international, but automatically we become global, united in one nation of Sahaja Yogis, where we understand that we are all part and parcel of the whole, the microcosm becoming the macrocosm.

All these things are easy if one understands that you have to be humble about it. If you are arrogant and if you are still conditioned about whatever you had in your past or feel guilty, then you take more time to grow. The best thing is to be the witness of what has happened to you, what you have been, from where you have come and where you have to go. There are so many beautiful Sahaja Yogis that once you start seeing them, their lifestyle and their behaviour, you definitely develop a feeling of using them as your ideals.

In Sahaja Yoga there is no force used, only guidelines are sometimes given strongly. One knows oneself what is right and what is wrong. There is no need to tell one to do this or don't do that. If one starts doing anything wrong, immediately one's cool vibrations indicate this is wrong or sometimes they stop also. So the best way is to depend on your vibrations. But to do this, you have to be in the meditative mood to feel the vibrations all right. Sometimes you can misguide yourself with your intelligence. The best way is to be in the meditative form and depend on your vibratory awareness.

We do not allow people to be called Sahaja Yogis or to come into Sahaja Yoga who are not yet of the level where they can give Realization to others. They are still kept as developing yogis because they have to improve themselves to enter into this sanctorum of collectivity.

When you are enlightened, it is very easy to understand this subtle knowledge, but if you are not, then it is very difficult to put these ideas into your head, which seem artificial. Once you are realized these ideas become your own experiences, so we don't have to push them into you, to make you understand. The only way one can understand Sahaja Yoga is to be a humble seeker and then to get your Realization. You may be a king. You may be a great successful person. You may be a business magnate. You may be a great press personality. All of this is of no value because you have to know that there is one stage still left for your human awareness to achieve.

It is not an individual achievement. It is a collective achievement and it works in collectivity. Supposing a nail is cut out of your finger, then this nail can never grow. So you have to be in the collective and have to become one with the rest of the people. Then only you will achieve the results better, like in a garden every tree which is growing has to help the others. Although it may not be done in the garden, it has to be done in Sahaja Yoga and it works that way. It is a collective ascent that is working out. Those who are not joining will be left behind. The concern is that such people who are capable of achieving it should somehow or other be convinced about the simple method by which this whole world can be changed.

Sahaja Yogis should never worry about money because we do not take money for our spiritual work and we always condemn people who are taking money in the name of God. Please remember that we are in the kingdom of God and that this citizenship looks after every need you have. You will get the experience of this throughout. Whenever you try to do work for Sahaja

Yoga, that money will come to you somehow – not illegally, not by force, but in a very miraculous manner.

CHAPTER FOUR

Sahaja Yogis

Sahaja Yogis are the people who have been enlightened, who have got their Self-realization by kundalini awakening, by the spontaneous (Sahaj) method. They are like seeds which have been sprouted whose living process in spirituality has started.

They are not Sahaja Yogis until they have felt the vibrations of the all-pervading power (*brahmachaitanya*) which does all the living work.

They are not Sahaja Yogis if they have not got full knowledge of their inner being, the inner instrument and the residual power of kundalini. On their central nervous system – that is, at least on their fingertips ,which are the endings of both sympathetic nervous systems – they must feel the all-pervading power of God's love and know about the decoding of their feelings on their fingertips.

The divine vibrations of this all-pervading power should flow all the time, but, if they stop, they should also know how to start them and how to raise their own kundalini – that is, how to be all the time in connection with this all-pervading power.

They should know about all the subtle things about themselves and also about others.

They should at least have the power to give Realization to others and, later on, to clean their centres so that they can give them physical, emotional, mental and spiritual beneficial nourishment.

The outer being of a Sahaja Yogi should manifest the inner peace, the divine compassion, the dynamism of ideals of Sahaja Yoga and a blissful life.

Sahaja Yogis become, as a result of matured growth in their divinity, innately moral, law-abiding, very honest, discreet, wise and extremely loving.

If one is not collective, one is not a Sahaja Yogi – that is, he has yet to feel his divinity, to mature so that he understands, in his awareness on his central nervous system, as an innate experience that he is part and parcel of the whole. This is the microcosm becoming the macrocosm. As a Sahaja Yogi develops his collective consciousness, he is very objectively aware of the blindness of his fellow men. He understands the true nature of the problem of his country and the whole world at large. He, with his divine discretion, understands and, with his divine power of love, works to correct the destructive, ridiculous absurdities, perversities and cruelties of his fellow men, his nation and world as a whole.

His concern is for himself and his fellow men, who are conditioned by modern exploitation projects into the new areas of collective problems. As all his ten valences (innate universal pure religion) are awakened, he develops courage to adhere to his ideas of Sahaja Yoga culture and emerges out of the condition of falsehood surrounding him like a lotus out of the mud.

He is bound by the divine nature of real religion. He is no more like other people who profess to a religion and can commit any sin against their religion. The Sahaja Yogi realizes in his awareness that there is proof that the source of all outward religions (even in deviated form) is one – and that is truth and purity. As he purifies himself with the living process of Sahaja Yoga, he finds the truth of the complete unity of all the religions. Thus, Sahaja Yogis may come from any religions or races, have no problem of fundamentalism or racism.

He finds reality as a very beautiful, blissful and miraculous thing. He, with divine grace, feels absolutely secure, peaceful and joyous.

His health improves immensely and he knows how to cure others with divine methods of vibrations. Gradually, he becomes healthy in totality. Also, he knows how to protect himself from negative forces, he knows what is right and what is wrong, what is truth and what is falsehood and he is empowered to enjoy the path of virtue and righteousness of Sahaja Yoga.

The Sahaja Yogi develops new talents to express his aesthetics, but does not use them to exploit others for his own benefit. In his business or any other enterprise, he has to express his enlightened mind, which is not selfish, mean and arbitrary, but absolutely follows his clear-cut ideas of benevolence. He enjoys the dynamics of his idealism, as he finds they produce immediate practical results even in the world of business.

Sahaja Yogis become absolutely honest with each other and they have tremendous mutual love, trust and respect without any expectations. Like many types of flowers, they realize that there are all kinds of beautiful Sahaja Yogis. They all enjoy various qualities, gifts and personalities of other people.

The Sahaja Yogis belong to one family and every member of the family, old and young or small, must be fully protected by the collective.

Sahaja Yoga cannot work out through regimentation, nor through compulsion, nor through force. It has to work spontaneously through the living process of evolution. In this process, once the seed has sprouted, the primule is like the kundalini which rises and, as the tree grows naturally, finds its way into the light. In the same way, a person starts growing spontaneously. Thus, manifestations of innate pure religion (Vishwa Nirmala Dharma) project into and outward from his personality.

Those who want to rise higher should not force others who are still honestly struggling with their lethargy, conditionings, egos and ignorance. Everyone must be given a chance to rise to higher levels of full potential by their own desire and seeking of truth.

But those who, after coming to Sahaja Yoga, are still, after a period, found out to be immoral hypocrites, arrogant, ruthless and cruel without any integrity, manipulating, thinking of money, those who can be blown with the fashions of indecent behaviour or dress, those who play into the hands of entrepreneurs, who use filthy language, flirting with men or women or having extramarital relationships, blinded by faiths without any proof or understanding, following cults and false gurus, superstitions or any such mean and low level practices, cannot stay in Sahaja Yoga, even if they come and try to establish themselves. Those who try to make money in Sahaja Yoga, who are marketing God, go out of Sahaja Yoga by the centrifugal force.

Those who are devious, the game-players who are in Sahaja Yoga, act negatively to sap the energies of other Sahaja Yogis, get easily exposed in the light of the Spirit, are automatically thrown out of Sahaja Yoga. Sometimes they are asked to leave Sahaja Yoga and to keep out for some time and, by keeping out for some time, they realize what they have lost and genuinely try to improve. Such people must be given a full chance again to come back with love. Some of them who go out, of course, may try to bring a bad name to Sahaja Yoga. No one should get worried or upset with their propaganda because we are now in the kingdom of God and all falsehood and attacks are not going to affect our growth or the growth of Sahaja Yoga as a whole. All such attacks actually react for our advantage, as the divine power is helping us all the time to bring the kingdom of God to this Earth.

Sahaja Yogis should not waste their energies with non-seekers of truth, but always try to help a seeker who is genuine, as much as possible, to seek the truth, with full understanding that he is still lost in a cocoon and he has to be very gently saved from all the problems he has created for himself by following false gurus or religions who are money-oriented or those who have lost their capacity to ascend into a higher realm, which is the main principle or the foundation of every religion.

Sahaja Yogis should not feel hurt or upset, as their roots are deep down into the divinity. They should be like seaworthy ships on the ocean of illusion.

All the great principles of divinity and Vishwa Nirmal Dharma must be respected and be worked out in the individual or in the collective. A Sahaja Yogi has every right to inform about the problem in your centre or in your city or in your country to the world leader, if you think that your leaders are not helpful.

Sahaja Yogis become very intelligent, penetrating into all kinds of areas of knowledge. They should know all about the scriptures and about all the incarnations, prophets, seers and self-realized souls of the past and should be absolutely equipped with complete understanding of the history of spirituality, how it has grown and has come up to this level of Sahaja Yoga (Sahasrara) where the last breakthrough had to take place. Moreover, they should find out all such people who are enlightened souls and have written about spirituality, about divinity. They should also enter into scriptures and find out all the beautiful truths which can only be exposed through an enlightened mind, so that the quarrels between the religions can be completely stopped by showing that all religions are born out of the same source of spirituality.

So a kind of plurality develops within a Sahaja Yogi and he respects all those aspects of religion and the people who started all these religions. Moreover, he should know how all these prophets and incarnations are related to our subtle centres. He should also know how he can awaken them within himself on his centres. This is all easily understood and can be practised within a few months and proven by experimenting on people.

The living process works in Sahaja Yoga. This is fundamental point one should understand, that the living process unfolds by itself and gives its own beautiful growth to the nature. In the same way, it starts working in the human being. Before a human being is enlightened he is like a dead seed which has no meaning. But, when it is sprouted, it starts acting and the nature looks after it. Actually, the nature is looked after by the same all-pervading power which is looking after the Sahaja Yogis who have now started their living process for the first time. As you will understand, human beings cannot do any living work. Whatever is dead, they convert it into another dead thing and they get into ego. But a Sahaja Yogi can very easily understand that he is now unfolding his powers and that when he uses them they grow much deeper and wider and they give him more confidence in whatever he is doing.

This faith is not blind. It is the faith which has been experimented and has been found out on your fingertips. You can know the truth which is spoken of in some of the scriptures. For the time being, you have to concentrate on improving yourself, cleansing yourself and then you should project your attention onto others who voluntarily come to you or ask for Realization. But never go from door to door to ask them to come or to beg of them to get Realization. There is no place for such people in the kingdom of God. One should pay attention to only those who want and are anxiously trying to evolve, because we must respect the freedom which has been given to human beings to choose whether they want to ascend or descend.

Keep yourself protected from negative forces and people who are negative because they feel challenged. As they have been carrying on with falsehood, they will get angry with you and they will try to harm you. As far as possible, don't advertise yourself very much, so that people will not attack you. Also do not get into competition with others or into jealousies. If you are a good Sahaja Yogi, you will automatically reconcile to your own life and you will not disturb others.

All the great principles of divinity and innate pure religion (Vishwa Nirmala Dharma) must be respected and expressed in the life of a Sahaja Yogi and in the collective. Sahaja Yogis cannot take any money for Self-realization or for cures through the Sahaj method.

If any money is collected by the leader, it should be reported to the world leader.

The household, family work or daily life must manifest special qualities of divinity, such as:

Truth; non-violence; divine love which is not possessive, but nourishing; respect for the respectable; respect for parents, elders and the law of the land; respect for art and artists; respect for all the scriptures; respect for all the religions and their founders; respect for one's chastity; nobility, generosity; self-esteem; courage to imbibe and stand by the truth; selfless efforts to spread Sahaja Yoga; honesty; righteousness (*dharma*);

balance in the centre; knowledge of the divine power and Sahaja Yoga; gentleness; sweetness; forgiveness; universality; non-competitiveness; satisfaction with spiritual comfort; dignity in dress, language, bearing and personality; assiduity towards meditation.

Sahaja Yogis are always joyous. They do not get bored. Sahaja Yogis have a sparkle in their eyes. Their faces are fresh like flowers. They are neat and clean. They follow a very meticulous system of personal cleanliness and the cleanliness of their ashrams.

CHAPTER FIVE

The Leader in Sahaja Yoga

To be leader is a much higher test than just to be a Sahaja Yogi because the leader has to be an ideal for others to follow. He should know and master all the knowledge about Sahaja Yoga, the modus operandi of awakening the kundalini, giving Realization to others with all patience and love. Because Sahaja Yoga's foundations are divine love and divine benevolence and if you are really earnest that the whole world should be benefitted, then you have to develop a beautiful loving patience to achieve the Realization of others and to lead others.

So, a leader has to have an approach towards other Sahaja Yogis in the centre that he leads from the heart and does not pay a lip service.

The leader should be a patient listener, not criticizing or jumping to conclusions.

The leader should have a quick understanding of the complex problems which are facing an individual or the centre.

The leader should know every member very, very deeply.

He should always try to find out why there is a problem and how it can be solved extremely gently, with care.

The leader should never rationalize his mistakes, which can be just a cosmetic appearance and not the truth.

The leader has to first face himself and has to purify himself so that his own purified life will enlighten others much more easily than giving lectures. So whatever are your precepts, they must be practised by the leader with great zeal and with great joy.

That means the leader should become first his own leader, experimenting all his beautiful ideas upon himself, so that he should know how he can manage himself before he tries to handle others.

The leader should be very active, efficient, prompt, forgiving, generous, respectable and loving. If he is not respectable, then respect cannot be demanded from the other members. The Sahaja Yogis will definitely respect him and trust him automatically because he manifests respectful qualities. The leader should never try to enhance his own credibility by diminishing that of others, but must always build up a democratic style of leadership that is a collective one and should not assemble "yes men" or coteries around himself and should not give way to false praises. In case of a problem, everyone must have access to the leader.

The leader must understand the process of growth, which is a living process that unfolds itself like a seed becoming a tree. So, forcing or manipulating will not work out the unfolding. On the contrary, it will hamper or may kill the living process. The best way is that the leader should also introspect and watch the natural process which is unfolding beautifully within himself.

If there is a storm or chaos around, just calm down, station yourself on the axis of peace. A leader must know that we have achieved a state by which we can put our attention absolutely on the pivotal point of peace, which he should practise again and again and master. The leader must, through his experimentation and the proofs he gets, believe as reality that we are now in the kingdom of God and the power of His love, the paramachaitanya, is completely knowledgeable and absolutely efficient.

Gradually, the experience of this divine love, which acts, makes a very strong group. They will lovingly adhere to each other and feel the collective force as a living energy. The leader should try to live and to be like everyone else, not to be extraordinary, knowing consciously that if you are ordinary, that is extraordinary – in Sanskrit: *samanyas asamanya*. Awareness is the source of your ability to lead.

So the leader must try very carefully to watch the growth of his awareness of things. It is very easy because you can depend on your kundalini, who will make you aware of whatever subtle area you want to be aware. You can achieve it by using your power to project your attention to whichever area you want to know about and it will work out. This modus operandi of your attention can be mastered by you as a leader and then you can teach all other Sahaja Yogis how to master this art of directing your attention through your kundalini.

The leader should not stir up any emotions violently, but delicately allow the emotions of the yogis to come up and allow them to calm down by themselves. If the Sahaja Yogis are heated up on some point and even if you know they are right in their anger, try to understand the whole problem and make a drama as if you are also angry with them for the same reason. You should not suddenly drop cold water on the heated minds, but, after acting with them, try to bring them around and cool them down, then sit down with them and coolly discuss and decide whatever is the best way of solving the problem.

The modus operandi is to know how this divine power is to be used, is to be manifested and is to be respected. The leader should not stoop down to get after or fight any one person among the group members because your weapon is the light of the Spirit, which is the ocean of forgiveness.

The leader must step back in silence and be gracious. Your silence will definitely calm down the fighting spirit of any angry group member. So the leader must know and master the skill of silence, which makes the divine power take over.

Sahaja Yoga is to be mentally understood and is practised by the heart. For some people it is the other way around. There should be no hypocrisy about the knowledge. If someone in the group finds out or experiences anything subtle, it should be listened to and very much appreciated by the leader and the group.

The leader should know himself and not indulge in sycophancy at any cost. He should not have any favourites. The leader should have his absolute values and divine experiences intact. He should never project them or give his own colour to them. He should not try to outshine the teachings of Sahaja Yoga and never entangle Sahaja Yoga in the network of words that is *shabdajalam*. The leader should not try to be spectacular or a show-off, but should be innately humble. If he seeks fame, he will be carried away from reality and his great task of the emancipation of human beings.

The leader should nourish his or her group and make all efforts to make every individual grow and also to make the collective grow in divinity.

The leader, when not able to handle anyone, should inform the world leader. Without the permission of the world leader, he cannot ask anyone to leave or take anyone back into the group.

The leader, in silence, can feel the content and the concern of the group and also the mood, like the seasons of the year. Sahaja Yoga is a living process, so it is to be worked out like an expert. Like a flower, if someone is losing one's freshness, then find out the root cause and help the individual. Sometimes the whole garden could be under attack, so find out the real problem and try to solve it through Sahaja Yoga methods.

The efforts of a leader should be to create an honest and an open group. His job is to facilitate and illuminate what is happening, having very few rules and taboos. Too many rules reduce freedom and responsibility. Moreover, enforcement reduces spontaneity. Remember that all of the people of the group are yogis. They are enlightened people. Manipulation will breed evasion. Every law creates an outlaw.

In the light of the awareness of the leader the group will grow as an honest, open, loving group, acting in a wholesome manner. Their behaviour towards each other, towards the leader and towards others in the society will be very peaceful and gracious.

The leader should be softly-spoken, but strong, like water which can cut rocks, but cannot be cut. The leader should know that we are all part and parcel of one unity, one body. Any harm anywhere in the body hurts the whole, so he has to be very careful not to take sides or hurt anyone who is yogi. All things which are against the whole create bad vibrations and negative forces build up and sometimes they might explode and become a very big force against Sahaja Yoga.

The leader should not fuss about food or comfort. He should express contentment. He should see joy in simple things. The leader should not indulge in any contest of eloquence, nor should a yogi be encouraged to pass blunt or sharp comments on others. Of course, subtle humour and sweet friendly mirthful relationships like "pulling legs" is to be enjoyed. Whatever is benevolent is good for everyone and not just for one person. If this principle is understood, then most of the things will become very much easier in detail.

The leader should follow Sahaj culture, which encompasses all the good and righteousness of all other cultures. The social cultures, political cultures, economic cultures, whenever they deviate from spirituality, lose their balance and their basic principles. They are not in the centre and so they will be thrown out of the circulation of evolution. Sahaj culture is in the centre, is dharmic and makes you ascend in your spirituality.

The leader should know about and respect all traditional religions, all the incarnations, prophets, seers and all the realized souls of the past and the present. They should be aware of these religions, which have been in their purest forms once upon a time and might have deviated from the right path. That deviation can be easily detected by an enlightened soul. The people who have deviated go into a kind of a conditioning, which creates a blind faith and a complete halt to the further progress of spirituality. When the religion is professing about one person, then especially it can create people who start despising other religions and criticizing others and finding faults with others. So whatever religion they might profess, if they are criticizing each other, they are just the same. One must realize that they have lost the sense that all religions come from the same source. They have only partial knowledge, which should be expanded and is to be verified through Sahaja Yoga.

Every religion has said that you have to have your Self-realization, your second birth, but these people can just brand themselves as self-realized or selected or elected people and can go ahead with their blindness into the darkness of destruction. That is why sometimes we are amazed how certain people who are professing a religion are creating a society which is completely decadent. Those people who just believe in the Father, the God, are all right as far as their economics and politics are concerned. They might also, after some time, deviate very greatly because, after all, it is a movement towards the right side.

Now, if they believe in God Almighty as the Father and not in the Primordial Mother, then they can commit sins against their mother and the sins against the mother are absolute immorality. Such people will find their freedom to go into all areas of immorality, which will give them all kinds of horrible diseases and troubles. One has to be careful. Before criticizing these people, the leader must tell the group to take a very benevolent attitude towards all of them because, in any case, they are getting destroyed. Try to save as many as possible by telling them what these great saints or these great incarnations have said.

Also, the leader can read books which are written by some enlightened people to show where they have gone wrong. They should not say that "I say so," but they can use some other book, like that of Kahlil Gibran or William Blake or someone like that to show how things were said absolutely in a wrong manner by some of the people, who managed to enter into the scriptures and master them.

The conditioning of religion, although people are educated, is very strong and the strength of these religions is not of morality of goodness or righteousness, but of destruction because they think they are the best and they try to destroy others. Sometimes when these things come up with such a vengeance, people lose faith in religion as well as in God, but a Sahaja Yogi knows that there is God. A leader, when dealing with such people in the presence of other Sahaja Yogis, has to warn the Sahaja Yogis beforehand that they should not try to jump to any conclusions and should not say things that will upset those people who are already blind and who are going towards hell.

If you take a very motherly attitude, you will understand that these are like lost sheep and they have to be saved with great kindness, compassion and attention. But in case it is too difficult, you should not bother about them. Leave them alone and maybe one day they may work out better because, if the kundalini has started working in them, gradually they will come around.

Sometimes the people who are lost in blind faith are never seeking their enlightenment or their second birth. Leaders should not force the illumination of such people because it is a big task. Instead of that, try to look after easier people who are earnestly and honestly seeking the truth.

If we understand that all the incarnations are coming from the same source through their inner divinity enlightening them, then automatically we will know that there is a higher life than just blindly believing in some faith. Somehow they should know the basic principle that all religions are the same. They came in at different times and they had to work it out according to the times – *samayachar*. Knowing the Self. *Gnyana* is higher than reasoning. Reasoning comes from ego, but absolute knowledge comes from the Self. The leader should follow a spiritual life, enjoying his spiritual values and his gnyana will grow more and more on his central nervous system.

The leader should enjoy his selflessness. He must speak in the third person. For example, he should say, "It does not work" or "It works." He should not say "I am doing this, this is mine, these are my things." The word "my" should be dropped completely from the vocabulary.

The leader should develop himself fully, but if he needs to, he can take help from the world leader. He has all the freedom that gives him complete responsibility to decide for himself. But if he finds himself in a situation where he needs help from any other leader or from the world leader, he should go all out because they are all your own, part and parcel of the one whole.

The leader should not be a money-oriented, materialistic personality. He should not be rigid, tough or aggressive or demanding about material things. He should not ask for money, but he should give away his things and his money as presents to people or to help them. The modern materialistic society should never be a model for a leader.

The leader should lead a very clean, neat and artistic life. He should also respect tradition in his dress and household.

The leader should know about the worldwide growth of Sahaja Yoga and whatever is taking place.

They should keep all the cuttings from the newspapers. If the media is criticizing Sahaja Yoga, then it should be noted. It is good, in a way, that we can see our shortcomings. If the media is not honest, one should not worry about them.

All successful experiments of Sahaja Yoga in other areas of medicine, agriculture, sciences, music, arts and crafts, literature, drama, poetry, business, education and schools, photography and architecture must be recorded carefully. They should be reported to all the city centres.

The miracles of Sahaja Yoga must be recorded and should be reported to the world leaders.

The miraculous photographs must be reported and shown. They should not be shown to people who are not seeking the truth.

There have been a few Sahaja Yogis who were leaders and who had to leave Sahaja Yoga. Some of them started becoming dictatorial and started making money on their own. Some of them had some physical weaknesses for some sort of carnal love and have also departed from Sahaja Yoga. But there are some who fell prey to their wives, who were not Sahaja Yogis and were nowhere near the quality of a Sahaja Yogi.

Such women have dominated their husbands for their personal needs and also dominated the group. Such women are like so many women, such as Mrs. Chiang Kai-shek or Marcos' wife. They are the ones who try to take over from their husbands by dominating the platform and want to assert themselves, while they have no capacity, no ability to be there.

The duty of a Sahaja Yogini who is married to the leader is first to understand that she is the mother of all the group and she has to look after the group with a very forgiving nature. Supposing a leader does not like the way one of the group members is behaving towards

Sahaja Yoga, it is the duty of the wife to talk to this particular individual and try to tell him in a mild and motherly fashion that he should try more to work it out and gently reach a certain understanding through his efforts, meditating and reaching his divinity.

It is she who has to look after the comfort, the food, the clothing and the overall care of the Sahaja Yogis. But instead, if she starts using them as her servants or using them for her own demands and her own wants, if she starts using their money for a particular purpose, then such a person is absolutely incapable of being the wife of a leader. Such a leader should immediately find out what this woman is up to and then he has to tell her very frankly that he doesn't like all these things happening and, if she goes on like this, he will resign as a leader. After some time, even despite his warnings, if she doesn't accept what he says, then it is better to inform the world leader and offer your resignation from the leadership.

We have had really very big problems with two or three such women who have been extremely immoral, selfish and also anti-God. Such women can become very popular to begin with when they want to increase their popularity and then they come back as monsters, on the group or on one individual. This is possible because they are not seekers. I feel that perhaps they have been planted there by some devils, the way they have been behaving and acting and playing games with Sahaja Yoga.

The main source of a leader's wife is her immense love and immense power to sacrifice anything for the group leader. While the leader may not be able to really devote that individual time for the group, she can do it. She should never report against any one of the Sahaja Yogis, but always for them and, if there is some danger, she can warn her husband. In any case, she has to know that it is her responsibility, first, to verify that the danger about which she is thinking is not only to her, but to the whole group. All such situations can be handled very nicely this way.

The children of leader are nothing exceptional. They should not try to assert themselves on the Sahaja Yogis. They should not ask for any special favours or be treated like some Prince Charming. They should really live like very, very ordinary people, doing the work of Sahaja Yoga in a very silent manner. They should not be in the public eye. They should be behind the public eye, working it out in such a manner that the effects of that can be felt, but nobody sees these beautiful children who are enlightened souls.

Leaders should not get into quarrels about the property of Sahaja Yoga. They should know that this property belongs to God and they should in no way claim anything as their own, which is supposed to be that of the collective. They should, of course, be fully aware of the list of the things that are collective and all things should be kept in proper conditions.

The accounts must be absolutely clean and clearcut. There should be no money collected without the permission of the world leader. All the accounts must be shown to every member of the society. All accounting should be done in such a manner that people should watch and see for themselves your expertise as far as the maintaining of the accounts are concerned and the honesty with which you have handled the money. The best thing is to give the money to some group of people who can be called the finance committee, who should look after it and decide where it should be spent. Of course, the leader should have the overall charge of the money.

One of the weaknesses of human beings is money and when they start seeing money they may try to take advantage of the human weaknesses. So a leader should be quite aware of people who have still got this lingering weakness for money and should try to put such people into places where they do not deal with money. After some time, with their growth, they will become extremely honest people.

A second weakness human beings have is for women or men. This can be overcome by the practice of Mooladhara cleansing. If the Mooladhara is cleansed, it will improve a person who has this kind of weakness. But if there is somebody with this kind of weakness, please ask such a person to go out of Sahaja Yoga because one bad apple can spoil the whole box of apples. But even if it does not, it can create a problem for all the men or all the women who are living in that ashram. So a man who is a flirt or who takes to women very much, such a man must be kept outside the ashram. That is the best way to save yourself from the difficulty of handling people who are still not matured enough to be celibate.

Celibacy in Sahaja Yoga is that you live with one wife and with full confidence and it also means that you have to be with one wife all your life without even looking at another woman. That is the aim of Sahaja Yoga in the future.

Actually, this kind of attention, moving all over the area of women, suddenly recedes back into yourself and then you start seeing the good points of your wife and you want to lead a very good life. This happened in the case of Carl Jung, who suddenly became very friendly with his wife, absolutely attached to her and this must have come about because he became a self realized person.

CHAPTER SIX

Sahaja Yoga and Children

There are so many children who are born realized and are born to yogis. They have chosen their parents so that the parents can understand them and their style of life.

These children are like small, tender sprouted seeds or saplings. In our group, also we have children who got their Realization after their birth. Also there are children of yogi parents who are not yet realized, but are born very negative or become negative because of other relations in the family like grandparents, aunts, uncles, etc. This type of children should be kept outside the group, with the parents, if possible until they become Sahaja Yogis. Children, even if they want to, should never be forced to keep away from the parents.

Such realized children are to be treated very, very lovingly. Children understand love more than anyone else. But every child requires guidance, as they are to be citizens of God's kingdom. They must know the protocol of God Almighty. They must know all about the divine power and divinity. Children must be told they are yogis and they must be respected. With respect they will be conscious of their state of being and their honourable personality. The parents have to know that these children do not deserve any punishment because they are very intelligent and loving children. If you have to punish these children, then you must know that you have not yet proved your love to them because to them the most important thing is your love. If you tell them that if they do not respect themselves then God will be angry with their mummy or daddy or that they will lose their holiness, then immediately they will change their way of behaviour. They cannot tolerate any punishment to their parents and even to their leaders. If their parents fast for one day or miss one meal, that is also sufficient for the children to fall in line.

There should be a complete rapport with these children. The parents or the leader should try to be like them and talk to them in a manner as if they are of their own level and make them aware that they need their care and their help.

People mostly give lots of toys to avoid the company of their children and to avoid facing their children. Why? A Sahaja Yogi child is so interesting that you should really give them very few toys and enjoy the toys with them and have very interesting talks with them.

Never leave the children unattended in the compound or outside. There should be a constant invisible watch on them. You must know all the beauties and subtleties about them. The Sahaj children are the precious property of all the groups of the world. The parents should not bother if the child spoils the carpet or something of material value. They should worry more about spiritual and aesthetic values. All their creative work should be respected and must be encouraged and what they are about to create should be understood.

These children are so intelligent as to know how far to go with the parents. Most of the so-called wrong or bad things they do are to attract the attention of the parents or the teacher. This is, of course, seldom the case of born-realized children.

The Sahaj child should be allowed to use his freedom as much as possible, but he must learn to respect the elders and the boundaries of Sahaj moral life. That is possible if the other people in the group respect the elders who are very respectable. Immediately, they follow good things because Sahaj children are very quick to know what is respectable, so they very naturally follow what good manners the elders have.

If they pick up from negative children and if they are using bad words, you need not be worried about it, just don't pay attention to what they are doing and you will be surprised that, when you completely ignore them, they will come around very well.

All the good qualities of the children must be praised publicly and whatever is wrong with them should be talked over privately in a very gentle manner and they should be told that, if they behave like that, then everybody will laugh at them or will despise them as bad people.

The children should be put into competition of goodness, like sharing things, caring for each other, lovingly looking after other smaller children, competition in their wise decisions. The parents and the teachers must talk to them about Sahaja Yoga culture.

Children should learn spartan habits without in any way degrading them, hurting them or militarizing (regimenting) them. The best is to show them by the life liked and followed by parents and teachers. If they indulge too much in comfort in childhood, they can never be happy later on if they do not get comforts in life all the time. If they are kept in spartan habits in childhood, it is very easy for them to adjust to any kind of hardships and any kind of life they have to get into.

Children should be kept in contact with nature. They must know how nature works smoothly and gently. They should know about all kinds of plants, flowers, trees, vegetables and crops. They should play outside and develop the immunity of the Mother Earth.

They should know the different soils and how one world was created by God with all kinds of varieties.

They should know how the seasons are caused and how there is a divine control over the nature and how animals are under the control of God (*pashu*). They must know about animals, birds and fishes.

Above all, they should know about evolution, kundalini and Sahaja Yoga. They should know the practices of Sahaja Yoga. They should be made aware how they are born in these days of resurrection. They should be shown all the miraculous photographs and asked for their comments. Also all their miraculous experiences must be noted down.

The curriculum of the class must be followed, but in the spare part time should be given for expanding practical knowledge of how to use their hands (according to the *Basic Education* by Mahatma Gandhi). Also the personality of the Sahaj child must be expanded in other areas of music, dance, art, literature and eloquence. Thus, the vision of the child will improve. In any case, the child should not be burdened with books.

First and foremost importance must be given to a child's health. They should be checked once a month by a Sahaj doctor. If anything goes wrong with the child, utmost attention and care must be taken. These are precious children in our trust.

The food should be simple, nourishing, interesting and tasty. It should have variety. All should eat the same food, except those who require some special diet. Their attention should not be wasted in asking what they would like or how they would like the food. On their own, if they say something, it should be noted and attended to. They are very special, but their ego should not be pampered. They should be made aware of how to be respectable and well-mannered to prove that they are specially normal and ordinary.

One must watch very carefully the moral behaviour of the children. Until the age of twelve to fourteen years, there is no need to talk about sex. If necessary in some cases, then it should be done very privately, keeping the honour of the child. There should be no sex education in the open or in the class. It should be done privately by the parents or by the teachers when children reach the age of puberty. Their innocence must not be disturbed by very long explanations or open talks.

The personal hygiene habits of the Western children, especially, should be changed. They should not wash their face from the washbasin, but with clean running water. They must brush their teeth with a herbal toothpaste, like Neem or Babool, after meals. The tongues must be kept clean. Eyes must be washed clean. The nails and hands must be cleaned after every time they finish playing, after using the toilet and before and after meals. They should not use paper in the toilet, but lots of water. Every day they must be given a good oil massage from head to foot and in India, they must be given a bath every day. All the clothes must be changed into newly-washed ones. Hair must be cropped and combed with a little oil for boys and girls' hair must be cleaned and oiled a little bit and made into proper plaits. Shoes and socks must be comfortable and clean and feet must be kept very clean and protected.

Proper reports as to the aptitudes of every child must be maintained. Parents should be very much aware of their progress and their problems. A parents' complaints book must be maintained. The teachers should be Sahaja Yogis and have to be well-qualified.

They should be aboveboard. The finances must be kept by someone who cannot spend the money. The financial reports must be audited every year.

These children have to become great people in the field of human ventures, so all of them are to be prepared.

The main thing is to love and respect, which should be the foundations of the school. Regimentation is not needed for these children, as they are already awakened. The unfolding will take place spontaneously, but gentle guidance must be executed.

The collective behaviour of the children is to be very much encouraged.

There should be an exhibition of their works of art, their photographs and of their visits. There should be three months of holidays.

YOU HAVE READ THIS BOOK

NOW SET IT FREE

SHARE IT

SEND IT ON
TO BE READ AGAIN

WHERE HAS THIS BOOK TRAVELLED?

Write your name and city below.
Let everyone know where the book has been.

NAME	CITY

MORE ON THE NEXT PAGE...

More books with the words of
Shri Mataji Nirmala Devi

Anant Ashirvad: Eternal Blessings
Anant Ashirvad: Infinite Blessings
Ashram: Symbol of an Ideal World
Attention: Foundations of Sahaja Yoga Book Five
Collectivity is the Place: The Nature of a Sahaja Yogi
The Creation: Foundations of Sahaja Yoga Book Four
Declaration: Foundations of Sahaja Yoga Book Three
Dharma is Your Sustenance
The Divine Cool Breeze Magazine
Education Enlightened
Every Day with Shri Mataji: Words of Guidance and Wisdom
Foundations of Sahaja Yoga
Humility: Sahaj Qualities Book Four
Innocence: Sahaj Qualities Book Six
Introduction to Innocence: Forty-Nine Things to Know
Journey Within: The Final Steps to Self Realization
Joy: Sahaj Qualities Book One
Knots on the Three Channels
Love: Sahaj Qualities Book Two
Meta Modern Era
A New Era: Foundations of Sahaja Yoga Book One
One Hundred and Eight Questions
Seek & Ascend
Seventy-five Doors: the Wisdom of Shri Mataji Nirmala Devi
Sahaja Yoga: the Words of Shri Mataji Nirmala Devi
Shri Mataji Tells a Story
Spirit is the Goal: The Only Eternal Thing Within Us
Subtlety: Foundations of Sahaja Yoga Book Six
Wisdom: Sahaj Qualities Book Five

www.divinecoolbreeze.com

Lightning Source UK Ltd.
Milton Keynes UK
UKHW021313160223
417129UK00019B/591